Hymn to the Prisoners
of the Wasteland

GEOFFREY MARK MATTHEWS

PEREGRINATOR·PERENNIS

2021

Published 2021 by Perennisperegrinator
27 Roman Wharf, Lincoln, LN1 1SN, UK
Email: *perennisperegrinator@gmail.com*

Hymn to the Prisoners of the Wasteland
© Geoffrey Mark Matthews 2021

Illustrations and cover design
© Geoffrey Mark Matthews 2021

ISBN 978-0-9932054-9-1

CONTENTS

INTRODUCTION

I wrote this poem during the Covid-19 pandemic. To a large extent I am going to ignore this context in what follows. That may be perverse, but to be honest I am fed up with what the moment entails and in the long run it will not matter. When future historians get their heads around the facts they won't need any from me. More importantly, *that* virus is not what *this* poem is about.[1]

To say that a poem is 'about' something need not suggest a definitive topic or concern, one decided in advance of the writing, and it does not in this case. Insofar as I had an 'idea' at all for the poem, it was an idea about procedure and possibility not content. You could say I knew *how* I wanted to make the poem and I contrived to power this making with naked *anticipation* or, to put it literally, I took care of the poem before possessing it.

I brought a 'poetic' into play—that much is certain—and I chose particular wordhoards from which to select the material to work with. All the sources used are referenced in the Endnotes, which also contain a few diverting asides. The divisions of the poem broadly indicate the order in which different sources were used: *RSA Journal* → *Greenpeace Connect* → *Museums Journal* → *Being Human Festival programme* → *The Big Issue*, not that the content of each source matters too much; each section rapidly evolved its own momentum and atmosphere that to some degree fed off earlier and carried over into later work.

My thanks go to Colin Davis, Val Huggins, Dave Kenyon and my sister Catherine who all provided valued conversation and support during the year. And I particularly thank Mike Blackburn for his critical nudges when I was writing the essay that forms the Afterword to the poem, and Gilbert Adair for his notes on the first section of the poem and on some earlier experimental work. Gilbert's insights helped me sustain my efforts both in terms of method and of feel. Further than that though, our online discussion of "language in the reality-making operation" proved decisive in the inception of the poem.[2] He prompted me to read Alain Badiou's essays on poetry in *The Age of the Poets*. The reference in 'Poetry and Communism' to Pablo Neruda's Spanish civil war poems caused me consider why there is rarely anything overtly political in my poems. There are further thoughts on this in this book's Afterword. But now I think it is time to let you onto the roller coaster—remember to breathe.

26 January 2021

PART 1: ASHES OF THE OLD ³

He who was living is now dead
We who were living are now dying
With a little patience [4]

1
Hinge pop
would the form
of authentic prediction
will such stores a fail way
with experiences value fact
pleasure contact even surprise
memory increase possible visions
that belonging might
cut perusing people into
instinctual lives   not of denial
aimlessly grabbing yet
functionally dangerous
down the typical course
unparalleled conversations
all visit   all centre

I think one's feelings waste themselves in words, they ought all
to be distilled into actions and into actions which bring results. [5]

2
Hinges contest non-centring
change a norm
in development
particularly take
effective themes
just wisdom space
convening Oceania
attract portable ideas
low-health accelerators
to us in   place-work

In Oceania at the present day, Science, in the old sense, has almost
ceased to exist. In Newspeak there is no word for 'Science'. [6]

Comes on mid-western coast way
keen September of prompted outlines
exploring addition in this city network
resilient sign systems in spirit-led decline
meanwhile more time to place anti-models
in real narratives   and alliance

Scenic Africa at oil sales
past unleashing
power example
answers urgency
utopian urgency
how emergency
grows in rising   bears

3

Lone guitar
next axiom
in reset principles
identified privacy centres
to index common capacities
dementia models in mental rush
hence
consider metrics
and demand insistence
surpassing passive tracking
traded in core trust retirement
well brain
the pivotal human
requirements include these
intangible towers of intellectual
access   to need

Beaming tool can impair fluency
maintain the
fixed free portion
with face firm for quality
developed when beneficial arrest
is posited
scaffold of low living
especially child aligned
interventions that optimize entities

return specific
philanthropy   to dementia
units could   rage and
should bond   private brains

A tribal panic
modulated pursuit as
attached re-imagination
together   critical brain
                                   tangible brain
                                   digitised brain
isolation for   lost dementias
lifespan of   emotional brain
brain taken

Come Theban irony
choices that
allocate certainty
geared in drive shifts
surrounding stable norms
would harms include the future
has light   the looks

> *the God of Plague*
> *Hath swooped upon our city emptying*
> *The house of Cadmus, and the murky realm*
> *Of Pluto is full fed with groans and tears.* [7]

4

Never taken both coins
amplify signals
mechanism's pedagogy
build integrated exclusions
in lifelong
limited purpose
self-advancement
focus around formal stages
leave out required fiasco
deserve a making tone
strong fabric action
assessing ignored
technology   confusing

slap-up meals
with understanding
holiday   consequences

Pooch viol costing 1s 9d
number
toxic children
anxious children
severe entitled bodies
estimates of vulnerable
periods of absence while
2020 raging our office tablet
a discrete
central covenant
together between windows
together
in a rainbow   surprise

    ... it is likely that the civilizing process will manifest itself in other forms of violence. [8]

5

See pattern then any furtive moth born
antagonism
vulgar green today
respect reflected in spiral modesty
search poor inflated cities
pay explosion benefits
literally higher along
learned   neighbourhoods

Fauve holo-theme
extravagance begins
takes this special living
which zoning thousands
values talent
values shipping   value

Aye nations found dust
faceless symptoms suffer
what pertinent cycle
segregated so
battle collapse clear

in willing dream realm
poverty location between
incredible information shell
of vacant   living

Thought-voices are part of who I am, and what
makes me unique. With what will I replace them? [9]

6
Subtle idea ruling fire unit
essential generations
overhaul significant
rural expenditure
middletime ever
amounting to
boundaries
that start   changing

SOS is lax prop
emerging shifts
from tied stock
form frameworks
for parallel need
transparently and
swiftly
alignment
on consensus
levels its loss of
indigenous emissions
need and value   regenerating
detriment   entrenched
activities are perverse
or despoiling instruments
short as deliberate incentives
in nature bringing trade-issue as
effort-setting pressure
this to help play
decision mechanisms
solutions calling on
the complex ways
and questions   that change

Theatrical moon couples fanatic
false resources
tackle pressing risk
for the study preserve
heavy habitat of fertility
once our dependent affect
returns as tenable sectors
think of higher systems
withdrawn platforms
separate destiny is
looking by   upper review

That's genuine froth
ideal footprint amid
growing intervention

> *Mortify therefore your members which are upon the earth;*
> *fornication, uncleanness, inordinate affection, evil concupiscence,*
> *and covetousness, which is idolatry:* [10]

7

Mad most duped
time theory does control   why
but in deficit
has further
constraints
to labour
this limited
currency and
provide nothing
formulations bring
rising alternative wrongs
flawed predictions underlying
public religion which
many predicted
and a dedicated
if predictable   Daniel *saying,*

> *I saw in my vision by night, and behold, the four*
> *winds of heaven were stirring up the Great Sea.* [11]

8

Setting up other bank
widely will machines
be forced to fixing
democratising fairness
the disempowered balance in
model visions once consistently revoked
representations existing first
as private combines
static combines
of liberty of
host shapes
regulation's   certain origin

Rogue brain had me catch
existential scoop
the south compound
might be a zero-less spiral
farmers' fragile third collapses
the subversive activities matter
in flawed personalised logic
leaving mergers deemed
the ultimate cultivation
within harvesters law
path talking system
actually static reality
tolerated within the fast
concentration example the
handsome force that may have
stepped things   down

Kent is near wall
matters become colonised
a stock box of fixed efforts
responsible agenda
piling products   voluntarily

> *Not suffring forraine Lawes should thy free Customes bind,*
> *Then onely showd'st thy selfe of th'ancient Saxon kind.* [12]

9

Women rerun haven goals
works prevent a
long-centred everyone
Jones argues is blackable
advocacy-building approach
accumulating the dominant
extraction fight to better dismantle
inequity   and suffering

Quaint deity as cool hilarity
cooks exposure
of severe systems practice
exposed as their urban march
for sorted heads   half mandated
the possibility that   program owners
like trying   monthly
aftermath   surveys

Devon backing queer mentality
fewer people dream between
maintenance process and
agency perpetuation
than according to
expropriated
estimated
history
more
trace assets
rooted in how
net reality plays
throughout the day
explore systems   behaviour

Stay real for that idiot's coin quotes
would cotton conform
to wealth-ways primacy
source just north of
monopolised war
vertical slavery
formed of myth's   current pathway

Neat cynic eats liquid nation
return today to
typical white insight
realise all troubling
consequences fall
among the   denied

Tot of hero matter
significant roots are
exposed   widening

We don't know where they fit in, we don't know who they were,
but we do know some of them hung around until fairly recently. [13]

10

OK load a hinge
willing shock   the solidarity close
willing bright   firm with
disagreement
instruments have   deficiencies
yet time
controls
rising of
rooted will   over reason
exacerbated   transition
could contribute
divergence money
fostering disparities
materially while likely
process times   its effects

Curious jury fined feeding wet navy
borrowing
component also
borrows proposals
proposals reshuffled
among unprecedented   of the self
involving four sovereign
affected called Emmanuel
cohesion of extraordinary
poverty in health the time
faced consolidation crisis

functioning popularity become
Europe the high level current
above good support
as capacity clearly
repeated view   struggle

I analyse miniature addict's prime oils

past weak capacity of rescue games
in a common role to bond
because feeble
bank on sceptic   calm
limit emergency   measures
in fallout areas to
additional unused
delaying resources
and coordinating still
rationing unanimously as low
          constraint

I parent, I medic defend that thief

their massive disparities
prone to higher installation
remotely compared segments
about professionals' declined
occupations   lower last
raise advance
varying beyond
private indicators
significantly weaker   such
Bruegel distress first   rules
second sector states

> ... *being threatened with so many and vicious illnesses,*
> *as the Catholic evil, the gueuz fever, and the Huguenot*
> *dynasty [Protestants], mixed with other vexations* ...[14]

A topical splits

harder heart precludes
anything desirable   almost
towards cashed in   woes

I see I hate a quintillion cues
terms below convergence
more surprising to youth   declined
now a power example
suffers the elsewhere   lower

Win a solar deity
differentiated   before
fostering   will
devastating   corners
throughout   history

11

I give yon coinage verve
why question argument response
when needs mean practical embraces

Soot-soaring rust loss
misarranged mailouts   targeted
at writing barriers
benefiting life   support
as lifted fears   during
certain disabled
effects in a single   vision

Refresh pure rusts
investment
findings of
concern to   workers
autistic schemes
reaped for landmark
focus within unexpected
figures from barriers among
accorded dogged-for   challenges

Scalar sea scale
nothing   once
inadequate   overall
will persist for
June-age despite   renewal

… your social use maybe isn't quite what you thought it was. [15]

12

Mustard gas blew Hibernia head twice
risen tyranny had gatherers in darkness
described by lack-time economics
and anti-flourished sciences
in free-skewer practise
what envy threat
that startlingly
earns some memory
grounded in world capacity
finely armed and   limitless
coerced in a
deeply physical   tradition
since false assaults   on
the road from   health
reclaim
utopian doubt
from hobgoblins   in short
the terrified
hence the   noted
factors   exchange
prudent   fires
like play
with
flames
that speak
of further fight
taken in evidence   I believe
failing good dealing   humanly
thinking real threats
condition ordinary
word music
among
accelerating
long-poison times   being
in language   word-breath
to listen after poets laugh
in images which are the   chemistry
they disdain
discipline
the age shift
couple the scribble

called supplement and
thrown to you approaching
the varied outline of naughty   snow

I'll put a girdle round about the earth
In forty minutes. [16]

13

Laugh into any finest do
wonder at
imaginaries
individual rising of   care and
ultimate becoming in   thought
alerted to voice   and complex
of deliberative   stripes joining
experience
practice
years
of
protest networks and
minimalist culture and
fire in the imaginary   divided
for seeing initiatives
distribute toxic   goddesses
and often   to inspire

See famine with an iron greed
end   beginning in hope
art   edict or trope
located   shy types wait
easy   not clutched

Try idiotic pout CXV
derangement of heart
alone eating into wild blocks
to boost habits and immorality
positive time of thought-cost
in lacklustre performance
affirms unfit treasury
infected with recent   fish think
this kind inspires
by adopting   irresponsible

people to
imagine   transformation
is repeated   to get toxic

Not gross demands
bounce
contraction shaped everything
in desperate pocket work-out
imaginary moment moved
from uncivil intuitions
in the translated age
to slice powerful
imaginary monopoly
melding cultural tools
buccaneers own excess
holds unseeable fun glue
rational Sartre to mediated
medieval solidarity   seen
                    in monsters

A halade a halade! [17]

They come in gaining more
nothing
one spoke
of any reality
escapes decades
of the vanity bubble
millennium virtues
effectively call
lucrative
only   grotesque media
which reason
pointless hyper-sexed
argument for enlargement   feed
breakdowns ahead   insane things

14
Catch the racists save time
creating speakers
illuminate and
make vital   perspectives

| catching | for |
| part-strategy | founders |

But I have no democracy and the democracy
I haven't got Hitler did not take from me. [18]

15

Last day's war act

updated	times
allocated	project kind
scaling live	alignment
in make-out	of futures

... a necessary dilemma in conceptual and historical
terms, set against the western proposals for logic
and its modernist aspiration to cohere ... [19]

16

Arty with a glad pop

found	
how the	critical
foundation	
is equitable	
given care is	
the problem and	
three little cultures	
maintain their one head	

I do not want to write a palindrome. [20]

17

war stunk of more refuting froth

pilot helps	
early Beuys	change via
background of	transition to
entertainment	
surprisingly	viable
forever and	
explored in	futures
automation	
where risks are	accommodated

18

Spice rope
imagine disorders missed agreed times
of loss   the philosophers describe

Or threads
mortar solutions   make cohesion
write   shows

Demure maid
brain-ways   catch
historical   discussion

Or angled
into   imaginaries

Its emotional mode of appearance is the uncanny
and the fear of going mad—two themes that are
not the exclusive property of romanticism. [22]

19

A gift to relieve us flat-footed crooks is trouble worth a rue-world
cheerful content of premature words
only an orthodox vein to fascinate
the taken of global form before
our good work be
underlined in lives
the idea craft parcels
in frail gas-shift glass
full of bold ashes rising
in disruption to have high   regards

Why do you not do as I do? Letting go of your thoughts
as though they were the cold ashes of a long dead fire? [23]

PART 2: VIRIDIAN MERIDIAN

In memoriam John Russell (1954-2021)

Perhaps we can say that every poem is marked by its own '20th of January'?
Perhaps the newness of poems written today is that they try most plainly
to be mindful of this kind of date? [24]

1

Haughty cultural [25]
Man did not fall … he stood up! [26]

This world from which we take everything
is the shit we're in to bury everyone
and why? … a little silence for the because
but the because
like snails' actions unearthed
come and save our   trails   travails   travels
from control tower controls
come and save our   be   *being*   beginning
why global all over the series
                              aerial   terrestrial marine
with everything
to report to Aves Mammalia and
swimming things of sea at dawn
before   diversity

un-legacy peace garden plaque
engraved as a gravestone in
contact with the way to … life in fact
generally understood
should best position
flowers of conscience
others had ambition years
yet others   had mindedness

what could not be grasped
so the social details and everything
fascinated Ella
well-lived in marigolds and

☼ clap hands

23

forgets the big waves that
balance Marcel of the field
on the balls
of both his slob-earth feet

2

Saint saves the jab opportunity deflects [27]
rights of destroyers responses
                    to powerfully influenced
Anglo-conquered lands   as promise and want
particular territories patterns   we understand
the burning character here
that Roman hybrid about
electronic readers with
large friendly numbers
involved in causing
              you know
                         a giant message
daily lives could contemplate
            much that participating involved
both of direct executive text
              and of the painter's damage
before the important ways
         are lost alongside the
              objects of communication
and suffered across   other listening times
though many have seen
          significant elements of elsewhere
argued   throughout our present

3

Now act [28]
shop
and our shelves replace chains
fresh
meat forever in the reverse choice
slave
destroyers need to have this standing
              pivot
knee dance see they've outed sir at seed
veils

switch serve to eerie night movie off
sheriff
snail sail peer on selfish sea roads
POSH

untimely ripped [29]
      by forest
            promising
burning bright [30]
      still reared
            the king
cursory digit points
      to pushing
            the release
six hook by six hook [31]
      processes poison to
            passing pandemic
the drag on-end ever
      cramped packing risk
            cursory capped per mark

      like fed on shipped feed
deep fashion deaf defiling
      beef be burned a
demure Beeb is feeble
      vital driver of words
is dour over wire diluted
      causing the wonders
absurd to know earth is ok
      we threat their years
surrey air flutters through
      past animals in the midst
of diminutive vanishing laminates
      the control also rising
desires coleslaw lowered to knock
      and to burn events too far
a foot stove in a boot
      tube any vote stuffer re-
                  turning
      remote help with civil support
to poor Livius's superlative Homer [32]
      heritage is pictured but fighting

with knife the tub dirt keeps to jettison
        through years reached against
strength to cheer hairy Uther
        Pendragon pushed as ever [33]
reversed a ship nor guard
        earth who hears each aghast
                                    turning
        time jumped in recorded land
tunnelled head or keen image might
        for grabbing that smokescreen
near Hascombe stathes in bargain land
        used on eyes for an urgent think
a kith edges earner off cyanide so
        euthanized foreigner can sing
                                    turning again
        with closer wildlife
file to lie worse old Theo
        will habitats be done
new deeds scattered by Leo
        accelerating atmosphere released
to seal here reef some tangy *terre* elixir
        to survive we depend on the start
tarts smother in odd repeated viva suit
too savvy to taper bonnier thumbs to art
                        a last turning
to make the heart
make it complicated
why would the ground
rain where drains start
irreversible years are
enough to produce
a generation to
imagine …

A SOUR CHINTZ MÉNAGE
A ZENITH AMONG CURES
AMAZING TEEN CHORUS
MORE IN STAUNCH GAZE
THAN ONE MUSIC, GRAZE
GIZA, ENCOUNTERS HAM
TRACING MUSEON HAZE
RESCUING THE AMAZON

4

Nois[e] *iv* / No itatic [34]   1
$\wedge$ $\wedge$

the eruption injures us with some
weathered wood grimaces

in once placid north the prudent
water of *being* crosses nature
with will which centred
would all energy wound

focussing alone he
shows high winds alive

already we banish standards in the drier
to hold in a warm day
before power dies unchecked

then dress neglected
fetched together for the dawn side
he tried in the kick-starting night

before impossible sleep
words fell like heat from
the flashing experience

on or off we don't option such
pain in the severe base

it is utterly nature facing two courses:
the smooth or the resilient push

all struck vulnerable in that
volcanic vision
exactly showering what is
well-loved of 1976 [35]

it was with first lust a rifling look
saying to the under-pleased cook
by defence this supplement ends

5
The black art connect [36]

Start a tapeworm club and exchange body sound tapes. [37]

a)   Come and search for
           Nostos again for I
           direct a group you
           may care to join.
Little people, this is our
pastoral art: non-violent
bodies of difference that
speak of astonishing stress.
           Doing too much media
           fools don't note even once
           the discrete dissimilarities
           that alter great iterations
which is too much media to
eschew this communiqué; it
never yellows but remains
a well of fire for ever.

b)   Remaining decorated, see yourself certain,
           yourself stay in that unchanged necessity
           of sadness—irrevocable in survival the
           fibre forms an astonishing thread.
Evening's tradition is driving rain
experienced as event and force, an
underestimated account of disposed
patterns forever retained inside clay
           and knowing the longer game
           returning to make past events
           enhance the code in new decades,
           speaking clouds, signing the way,
pouring emotions like short preserves
to study the plastic background of
plastic nature with acquired zeal
to fuel your hope in anti-climax.

c)   Improving disaster could decline
           with the real, while revelation's
           sane spells might introduce

the right pseudo-balance.
Procedures of prickling glass
mirror conscience between the
mean of funny options and great
applications of alleviated superstition.
        Promises are praised while diving
        between interstices of business and
        visits dipping from a mile-high fuel
        the betterment of our intellectuals.
Their calibre is evident in their closely
regarded calling patterns which ought
to trouble some sedative hour when
dealing with the whole of the 'I'

d)   Along the chain fierce nervous activity
        happens earlier and, when over the
        ocean's noise, makes you need to
        mark ambition by human thumb.
The hydrogen God perpetrates the break
of voices and themes around the harbour,
the momentum and style of the whole show,
made stronger by gathering numerous surprises.
        Place our year-ship in thought.
        Include that space safely in the
        outstanding pressures out at sea
        like everything ram-wrought in life.
Sanctuaries support the sharper half of the
world, mapping our wildest lives through
reports, soon to become green, turning
a disappeared piglet army of millions.

e)   Set here, realize looney claims that magic could
        bluff wrong-headed hundreds, light the gas on
        exaggerated carnival sand dances. Anybody
        shifting miraculous things to your country,
speaking genuinely of river control, has ancient
nature relentlessly well used and vanishing. A
trifle shall be crushed, since quietly signed it
begins to bother leading changes, as if past
        influences then pledge whole-sided
        heart-warned material perhaps to
        the energy of ten investments

and black heat can be more
to the Moon than one ant shows
of recent craft. Springing so closely
Charlie could break a fraction short of
undulating animals by our reflection but why?…

f)

challenges

take hope

so futures

happen

6
Prowl Mild Prion Today [38]
toothpicks bamboo
bottles and beans
near zero versions
rather remember
all are burning

hear a forest destroyed
colourful during
showing
really
hope and love lost
will grow to the cause
stop-watched in the
dirty posted pages

pressure   reading
pressure   day
pressure   checks
our fantastic   find
invigorated talk
expecting actions
confident given trust
coming close and you
suffering someone   reasons
this present   move

the difference ship surprised
stories the people wanted

landmark stopped time
and will committed
upside lines that
take morning
to needed
scared   showers
scared   climb
climbing up   the obvious
before really peaceful years
on submarine song of
dawned dive down
our sanctuaries
help six big
forever   marine
living   marine
so what   show over
the seabed   sitting
since voyages met with the   secure

ultimately   forcing
proud black   phasing
and single   demands
to listen   filling up
pressure   operations
pressure   feeling
power and
appreciated   people
speaking to people
to return the idea
giving people a
real enough
revolt in   the action

again just defenders
damage failed decision
ocean's traffic over sands
end   serious   signatures
take   spoken   survivals
share   signals

plug these people amplifying change
protect our ancestor's futures

watch if enemies watch
watch the   water
the   earth
the   animals
so many   terminal
ancestors and   legends
why tar won't think the
heart   the
page   the
sands
still speaking
from the choosing   sands

drop them
the willing paradise promises
that won't change the final days
uniting is buying all the baby can
clean   from
occupied attention to birds
being a drip   from
following to Mars in march
as everything my impossible mother
and violate source
persuades   to progress
                                   to plan
                         to make it touch
taking place
the language we lose   she says
is already
lost in   the future

forest falls into   clearing
breathe the land   haze
sleep the land   life
see the fears   she says
focus on spent time
lead the thing I think
even   to   be born

complicit in the
most of our pitch   the sound
                               the sound

swathes of purpose
inside the rare sounds
surrounded by
our telling

that's how you focus well
referencing the sanctuary   within
calling the foreign to   work
touch our decision
you liken to
evening   efforts

devastate   like this
worth the with and the fact
a proper   point
erected over
the secured ladder
a sense that some nerves   slept
at every practised ask   together

phase-fired
warrior rivers   themselves
delayed headlines
fish unfurled in Paris   peaceful
eclipsed sands that see
increased resistors
make waves

two toxic drops
protect island cover
being with more than   thinking
and   white events
and   human laws
core Quakerism issues
this issue sparked
first to protect   a last vision

7
Trusty guest's log fire [39]
before the experience shows
our support continues
your world that

nothing helps
even giants with
new actions to hear
new meetings to keep
compromise what never
put our future needs already
a decade   in detention

Mature crown toots pale poetry

another coming   about
like thinking from
once the plan can to
before the can is gone
through organized talks
in enjoying another ethos
speaking about sanctuaries
applied to night crowd works

Let clusters spoil the real painting

growing reach to throwaway
calling and returning
to people we hope
keep fuel from
worldwide
going making
food right loose
saying our trialling
after pumped up top
reasons in the pointless
midst near slash revealing
doubt while virgin felt an end

Trusted forces into   site they amuse

made back means   acting forever
still linked to tasty   weight breakdown
of each responsible animal   just to give
somewhere torched or   half-destroyed
to increase the nightmare   out here
growing all   winging years

The trusted run later

desperately gathering   in our world harbour
with marine like time   the crew won't point
to mapping oceans'   last sure sanctuaries
too late now
      something already lost
                     pressures activity
that damaged our   channel plastic heart
breaking up during winning
                 in incredible tagging
travelling entangled to   turn warming waters
endangered by having   tangled up its power
make sure the world's past
      between the water
         and our still-knotted cause
sweeps through
      so much precious network
              that we begin

Spite bump

thank the dirty today to
      make over our only formal transition
accelerate the decade by
      pretending exactly this model switch
finally shut the world to
      the hypocrisy in this looney record
create to start destroying
      and make empty claims the most
its breakdown alone
      books without disappearing and
temperature is   the response in nature and
why wind entirely   together or blocked
shut down all overnight   practising when
together giants are tracks   and toxic

I recreate rage thus we moved hook

blame it   to turn relentlessly
since the last   past the beginning
worthless bank of strategy   a heart
black from the heat   the break collective
with nothing   but offenders
about to change the proud

ever-arrested environment
before preparing the barrels
to block his first February
flashed down
with committed increase
for the fires

www.Inamevaliddesk.org

the name is to act like a message
the letter a
devastated January
a common support   only sounds the flames
at least neutrality   contravenes the landmark
empty voices
are heard helping fish
away from the damage
to court the meaningful decade
long-projected to morning outlets
the guardian
first called change
his house but
my comfort is
the outside series
of winning drills

I novis

make challenges to the gallery
fall over the power
as usual be more   to stand on promises
exposing the fossil   together in your energy
addiction opportunities
fall away forever
and now it starts

... The martyrs call the world.

W B Yeats, Adam's Curse, 1902.

1
First admonishes riven
revitalise the push   that pool
heading like a
glass addition to parks   of curves
company objects as
interwar artworks   previously naturalistic
the black mocks
a new real   the pink bucket
that rope
crosses and captures   with precision
relatively involved
a mass of deco art   composed
in English style
transformed   movement improved
where worn
opportunity   resorts to ownership

2
Hut of good froth
conversation playing   through
past successes   joining on
which migrant theme   people's
fresh response
is alive to   just decision
even demonstrations about   such trust
turned free at
vulnerable engagement   is
an original enquiry and   content
awareness of
digital working
is changing the menu   for trust
a pleasant week
of daring focus   enjoys
relatable activities in

the most virtual of wars   and gets
novel shortages engaged
with roses and   its time

3

End angel blinder
to discuss will
the mix is   acceptable

Sad causes in cadence
by verbal measures
adapting your will
to touch space   for access

Unsticks grit
on being at
some surface
swapped out   found objects
open ways to time
it being best   to forget
each duration

Sucking dirt here
to follow low faces   from above
use bubbles of level   running
to distant places where
planned understanding
of key spaces and aspects   is
published online and
learning of their expertise
the gathered cut across   the needy

4

Smog now shout
visited our house
an excellent   physical journey
filmed in fortitude
some found restricted
share just one slider   immersed
in significant content
opened as a raft fight
expect our shape   our

high vision to
realise a theme
a lowered gallery   . . .
a half-gold launch

5
Shake silk for tolls
take invaluable parts   and age well
on mornings make   group time
to need care about   not
remote text range

Attracting dieting clone
help!
the valley section says   why can't
a wider group with
information listed
highlight hazards
which check out
the artist areas and
contributing need at
improved feeding tests
scan through transcribing   services
that platform fragile foundlings
for writing the beanstalk's one   match

Tureen trove of the rose mile
visit with
the remote   return to
museums

6
Basking rare brier
for weeks
a worked thing might
practice   a rejoining
process that needs a   beyond
introduces barriers to   difference
to invitation

Unlively thick sin
volunteering different   questions

as lower expectations   accord
with those implied by
science   with those
found in
research
as   in the race
                      for experience

Revived yester-call
apply new streamlining look
worthwhile ambassadors   process
target support radars
know that confused
thought is part of   their move

Fix bee bell
since working   suits
spare the recruit
project that story   right
of snapping army   lives

At our fiery floor
reports of York   allowed
training of
wake work   to
                        benefit
all sites of   workforce
organization
about their   resolve
                      to build

accordingly is
clearly our ask
and lacking   nothing

Live every first sounding
come practice   in most base
science   once white
                   we foster
more   rebuilding

7

And today is rich
a hidden real is man's
acknowledged passion
and the native greatness
of many erroneous British
provides an opportunity to
disregard a public restricted by
collections of glimpsed keepsakes
that show interesting and sharpening
points of   unrecognized stores
all are made with
stints of a limp sort
and deemed cruel by this author
man & boy   never offsite
I am geared   by little else   but books

8

And nowhere
replaying the seasons events
tree animations bring
fresh wonder slots   trees sharing
their virtual material
futuring the biome-swap   context

Munch tax note
offered within
familiar trees sliced
to top residual forms of
brilliantly powerful transparency
beneath the   nearby moon
explored arboreal drawing which
specific to the centuries
of striking stillness
photographs
regardless   of the section between

Fling at any eerie art
the solidarity question
is compelling
swaying   composition
            slightly long-filled

depicting depth towards
wandering weaving sounds
demands   described opening

At a broken cut
looking literal
with process perspectives
concentrating   on opening
              to chance experience
as our curbed relationship
could damage   among

9
Anglia thing wins a deist
expectation
challenges art
distinctiveness   nonetheless
clearly takes off
its compelling set

Wisp loads for me
attention   within
overwhelmed incarnation
staged expression from
intriguing connection
apparently looked
over a story here
a combination
of the late at   caused date
throughout   the late
features of   vital activity
to activity roped and revealed

Yo fry his shit
give display
the look of stories
with the greatest sources
imaginative local voices   overall
of thoughtful age
to crew years
including   adze spaces
played   proud through   brightling

Encash age
plan ...
while the playful
conjure airy highlights
the panorama has hurdles
seized by a sea of ambition
that stalls during its approach

                                   then

the relocated timeline
of an ancient quest   arrests
a local mouth in   laughter

10

Outlive Koran worry
hurry home world   for
immersed highlights   show
diverse criticism that
history had forgotten   shame

Swirl'd frost
protagonists provide   time
brothers triple peril
hyping writer of
the camera style
a reading that film   quits affecting
                           through
forerunner formats   another
                       instrument
has been back of peer stars   that
feels mechanical throughout
a narrative home   first
humbling millions   of things
with limited contrast
the difficult moving of
contemporary hammers

Oiler pine feeler
begin this piqued selling   life
and motion suggests   a remedy
entertaining matters   science sees
forgotten   role of right   in disaster fun

11

Surreal four-way tape hunt
discuss the   will
I inherited in
fortunate forests
before foreign   artists
               open

Poetry in arboreal show too throwaway to mount a lick
collaborative foundations

What makes you stand out in Basel
our founder's three industrial tryings
are most like preconception   free

New factual history does want lurch of us on pact video clipped
we preview masks online
to adapt august things
to work with what
could   be possible

Actual curly gel
foundation before
free contemporary music
selected against submissions
and features waves opened
for forward ambitions
complimentary art
former and over
opened before
set costume
and cancer   death

12

Clog stony area
art speak on another
unexpected thinking
phenomenal content
trust gone sense into
keen ecology speak
healing surprise
gasworks fact

by struggling
resources to
make sexual   and jumped

Unclean sex go chilling
can hosts
centre parallels
inside this collection   of thinking
chance black
dismayed   paid   to extend

Very misted artist
returned after collaborating in   museums pause
there hopes locate space   before truths
in being devised
like careful histories
in distressing remains
and on material fortune
edges of the world event
exist explicitly in internal   institutional...ing

Welt of chimes
during material emphasis
planetary connections are
a grieving response for
example strengths
across rapid
shapes in   forevermore
pivoting to
apparent ticking
the human dimension   is a closed
bewildering during this   well-up

13

Trust try a live cortical reunion
trials little trend   to
scope enthusiasm
quickly more works
surviving fingertips   online
to make important   offerings
from the archive   of ironwork

Love exits not licence
virtual techniques stabilized the condition
which sponsored Ireland's daunting material
ready boxes contain powers of patent impetus
petitions of original bureaucratic complexity
alongside extensive manuscripts of audits

                                                      at sea

French stop suicidal rage
with   surrogates across institutions
correspondence originals   lead the
replacement of   court transcripts
set private copying   into history

Star shine of Hermes
with trinity   head-quest lost
aristocratic   partition lost
300 landed
and imagined   that attached
volumes of augmented   work
produced the culture of seed formation
that boosted phased   hopes
duplicates relating to
centenary assimilation

Try wit rising hero
surviving life and   hole-forced
various incinerated   details
touched hundreds   of
opposed chunks
of consequence
battle chunks
of gyrating
seagulls   six   soldiers

14

Curing parish actor
from culture concepts   come
supported racist   rivers
shrunken after   each reach of
terrifying   conversations about
caring   encounters
causes   significant questioning   of means

Enact fangled human
night busloads of other
full-on cultures handover
spent processes   more about
missing materiality
than shifts in urgency
Australian anniversary runs
say systematic control is a
ceremonial track
a sacred institution of
unconditional questions   taking known
brokering phases to call   violence
intrinsically the driver but
visit   the visit   on *being*

Reason is uplift
unpacked
marina people
jostling grappling
and killing item keepers
also confront questioning voices

Arch of perhaps
a spiritual origin   it says connect
says time   this visceral offer
says be strong
where issues were   first secret
the generating fate of
dead supports expanded   to
encounter spaces between   documentation
to undertake place-severing   for   stalling

Note we approach a rain patriot
existential   break
over in confronting   soul
community coming   to midst

15
Aerial matings
buzzing tables
half relaxed in
tactile activity

craft together   contributions
including a concept   like
integral environment
it still feels traditional   yes
the weavers are always   well
their mettle is in   making
a national area   hybrid
with   under-words with   history

16
Mingled bed silks
show the potential approach
that painting offers to work
a daring thread-making effort

Being absent filet
find a reflected hoard
held in calligraphic bedrock
across from a static cotton mix
markerspace   it's a
rather embedded   club

Commit county inn once
wider spaces
in types as relevant
as hopes of trove
offering executives
soft science
next   an aspiring fox
                        keen to be branded
                        tells of revolution
                        sells its skills in
making sense of   depression
making models of   intention
in such awe   that
comfortable   curators
in such passion
make programmes   paint

Wow freaky now sing
growing status says   technology structures
            matter with

crucial discovery visits
               between
open offerings   and   modern offerings
that adopters
also converted   embedding
such access as
the picture   operates earns   untold income

Making space
the   foundation
outside of themselves
captures only fragile   kit
of the   privileged
a valuable
fellow founder
becomes a quality
on diffusion in York
on running in parks in   pursuit of
gendered house hackers   and
coding spaces providing   machines

17 [41]

Collar motion a bore
indisputable   lives
underline support difficulties
across their current tackle
postponed professionals
argue more control of
the zero green June   points

Teaching big plunge
last category weavers have
charity for artists' travel
thoughts ripple by
all across green   readings
actions stand   out   make
numismatic   military   queries
building   imperatives   and
hearts   mean as vital   founder

Act on ghastly farce
reducing champion zones   and

reimagining linking that   overwhelmed change
willing on real gas
share shape   starting between
strong blend   nick
the manifesto   issues   declared
have current   planetary
history stepped   advocates
concerns growing   real with urgent momentum

18
Post-rock fur power
winter data says   change hardship
to support the hub   and also
to join full steps and
        direct a march on   heritage
                        a healing resource
whose advocates make a
long eureka a form of trust   following
unconfirmed findings makes   *being*
the capture of the true   yet
by living where figures go   single
and time confirms slow releases
that heritage is found to be becoming first

19
Crowd long on skill
real ads   all reflected delays
worked proud people   seen
in head-long systems   to access
what the fresh adapts
to institutions occult   norms

High or free lip
the weak went following   wave sites
bubbling vast relaxed
measures in head   advantage
starting high holidays of   experienced
capture that the   buck
struggles with and
the system focuses
on other reported   swells

Night swine

the last
physically attracted   believers
spend less discovering   happiness
by carrying their domestic   benefits
and across all tool measures
to get positive
in all essential   experience
and delighted
in huge risings
about severely
tailored expectations
that overseas social trends   released
they bring sharpened children   home

Doors of sago

before enjoying   space
dwell in slots
operating to   protocols
position lines   engage
and expect a go-a   head

20

She pounds that art of pathetic grounding

all battles   understand statues   deeper ability
in openness   they might retain   this care by
removal of   outcomes & nuanced   realm or
huge enough   cultural head   removal

PART 4: IN A HUM SITE …
FLEA VISTA (A COUNTDOWN) [42]

Vicious age though it is for mirrors, it's the reflex makes the soul shudder.

*For about forty-eight weeks of the year, an asparagus plant is
unrecognizable to anyone except an asparagus grower.* [43]

They were in number as the weeks of the year. [44]

52

<pre>
                                        apply
                                 some human
                             but processed
                          touch to this
                       public level
                   of benefits.
               none of
           them, being
        hundreds,
is anything
to history
to classics
even to new
discoveries. The
innocents die before
an unconquered sun is born
and on … which work as well as when …
</pre>

51

… in wearing a sense of soundings,
they explore what pay invites:
the mortal media—based
on comedy where
any history found
naughtily coded will
feature your community—to
publish stories of mass migration.
from animals of power
in longest sleep to
human light a

creation
for your perception to change
and celebrate monstrous grants ...

50

... belonging to
seekers listening to street stories
lucid Lucia in the darkness [45]
    life explores this closure and
flees to Elizabethan prose—it resonates
    harp-like by tales of night in prospect
of riverside creatures in archive plays yet
    is unaccompanied second by ...

49

... second—might contemporary scandals
uncover a wonderworker's corruption to shame
this expert chair
and complexities of the
non-adversarial discussion
provide evidence on film that a
right Charlie
led by the barrier
to breach history gates.   but how?
and what does it mean
to open some dystopias
appeal to marish-night
collapsed from alien wick

48

performance   reimagined
secrets that find out drama
at this research
intercut with work
with ... contemporaries   formed
who by her weave
night become stalls
flash the new computer generating discussion
object ways with England celebrating secrets
ethics of their past chance panel   combined
in every family there are   secrets

bad little girls
give them
big bad boys
rediscover them
seldom journey this

47

giving thanks across ocean history
park making and
led by challenge
fasting ways of winter
writing a timeless drop through   immortality
which tells an
extraordinary modern medicine
hop performances through
personal research
hidden Kings
do art   it's personal

46

patients
illness
and a chance tolerance
lived core of celebration
patience making ancient   identities
across storytelling time
mysterious site
the performed poetry inspired by
evening
pop and memory
venue of speculation
might two world-making readers
endanger ... legend events
in contemporary   spoken residency
this we speak

45

think really as
stone-haired monster
is this snake-making hand at the
secrets of home   a piece on philosophy

discovering conceptions   we find
in a dizzy Moroccan music
and to learn in this beat-twist
silence of the eleven-beat discussion
for Joyce generations ground together
slaves in their untold campaign   performance

44

for ages
explorations state
the public standing in
participatory composition
walks expect our local sounds of
all their own Hallows-end memories [46]
to curate this event the images think
inspired by the world of humble   beginning
and incredible talk involved   was
part-truthful ...   imaginative
cabaret news
the science is Beckett and Brecht
appearances on hand from an informal ...

43

... share
ephemera bring their crowd-mapping length
and the grave abolition between
the hidden in exchange
and archives
standing alongside the   Celtic heritage

42

the politics of complex excavation
           shows its ice & fire
English sketches occupied by
          cabaret and pale...
placeless conversation overlooked
         yet *in the news*   *everyday*
the care mixed by women
         in the mix...
the enslaved first in foreign
         curated aviation

fascinating with its hour-long layers
greening power   of the   universe

41
for magical aspects exploring this day
throughout the night of poverty talks
the current late-milk cocktail of facts
                    reveals a silent keep
to create war stories
along to this death and dying taboo
drop from bite-building installation
a spectacular infirmary awaits you
packed ...   unwrapped

40
and lasting in habitat awareness now
make the life in question changing
that mean of secrets
poet bounce with
history underground
and in the town perform
the lively yesteryear locations
and decode a house visit   deceit

39
heroines of books will adapt...   and watch
in pioneering evil being
fed up with place
understanding
how mystery
ground both
above and   below
the secret why
what secrets among
their archives and libraries
pop up on human clips of themed   nostalgia
and bring persuasive arguments
this soul-cleansing day cast   as excitement

38

smartphone trails from chance   please
word-historical execution in extra-dark   equinox
along make up day the
human origins talk of
all their ingredient   animals
brought to life
cracking the graffiti codes of this day   see

37

data young people invited with
touching talk
like a pirate in the beach
through past family-humans

36

normative library look
dad doesn't age
son becomes brother is
artist's self-styled diversity
reflects grooming through
hammered nails
upholstery satin
saint stain and
get your part short
share express women
visit citizens or global …selves
people who discovering arrival   record
graphic   country   documents

35

jam such allowance   the answer
histories listen to drop
experiencing evil humans
how the strange talk returns
to the disappeared of evacuated
nuclear village histories of 50
secret wolves   unveil   material
you are focusing on this
multi-sensory collage and
between factory work their

rekindled migrant textile light
to bring will behind the screenings
through its overlooked   discoveries   of art

34

express your gain
              son of furrows
                        light the skein
cutting to consider family writing
                    ahead of the everyday
like artefacts mark the where your art pops from
                behind the unique reveal
teenagers swap stories
teenagers screening questions   provoking
                    C21st selfies
with a diverse   evolving   cast

33

son ages
throughout bone
           to bristle order
        across the plot lines
        collect a box to burn
          unfortunate anniversary of wildlife
throughout the banks
        of secret voices
      vibrations of the 'ether'
              Marian performance of
special collections
      memories and glass spheres
      or global books about
                excavation
        near days   of eight hands

32

bingo for lefties   table-diggers
estate an unlikely home
local mobility *in the last decade*   of night
the uncanny across autumn
followed by a short wrath   to celebrate
their shape

reflect the contemporary   madness
for the ballroom

31
both children of discovery prepare for Oswald's
con...   dis...   ex...   cretion
culture of moving yourself   the basics will
command   international building
have   a couple of harpist hands
              about the world
the fascinating robot   does the tours
with Sithney   and some Englishmen

30
footsteps tracing
                unuo libro
                              handwriting along
powerful conflict   spilled-out today
on medieval   ancestors
revealing   the town projections   by England
its   voyages commemorate
                              connected philosophers
the spots discover this
                    free and infamous derby
lived how and here
                    in archives around the world

29
mural masks the family craft
talks to theatrical banquet
and tastes the immersive court
replicated in dreams
to draw their family relationships
trapped on land
the form of Rome burning the tale
come around
and everyday life this laureate meaning

28

that time   and its intimate renown
in music   among the castle's drama of murals
counted this strange material
darkness   drawn-on the city
and explorers   then encounter
all sorts of capture
        through self-digital samples of
                                its revolution
started in   this storming

27

making and featuring   PRINCIPIA
perform speed-surgery   of emotions
during this peculiar evening
your memories bring the keeper   of these
informally observed kisses to   fear
history under
gravestones in   cast-talk

26

youngsters with   elderly features
exhibit a vibrant mix of   little known writing
unlock images to tell carefully of
                        the most precious blood lost
will this inspired hand of centuries
            collected and experienced
                discover the thousands of events

25

can her lived story   led by global legacies
learn the untold days   of a new generation
during the hunt   through histories
planting fairies   and   forgotten exhibits
palm a range   of passion for
Victorian medicine   and   district connections
electrify your precious   substance at
most curious   graphite games   yoga day
for   two Vikings   in York

24

world work   incandescent swan
its library
             powers historian differences
                         and discussion
the original consumption
                  of great house-born legacies
the first modern plaques
           to unsung midsummer
                     in the surfing city
the recently received   share of the canny
further into the   local rights

23

marvellous treasure and
                  pox of the perfect slurp
dance nouveaux art dances
                  the master tunes inspire
discover migration out from
                  the hand you create
as new stories at this   family resurgence
and learn from artworks
            through the same daily lives
                  these animals have
a late conversation
             on history and
                  sheep memories

22

Avoid all iniquity, oppression, and injustice, for it is
blood judgement; although it may not slay by the sword,
it kills by means of the will; nor does it take heed of evil. [47]

your poetry in hieroglyphs
passes on   afternoon secrets
                  through their extreme rarity
           and planetary depths
          hidden the in music
                 of a Boniface and
unnerved escape
when as lies   by secret plans

then capture
        a simulated brilliance

21
for ages
        where true self is the journey from birth
the modern   is set against the story
of infamous purpose
of the new adventures   on towel day

20
expect one hundred   in the hunt condition
collage self-place and prose
        for poisoned hot assassins
and through medieval use
        delve into beautiful materials
bee years and
        cave paintings
        get this in hand

19
responses to the writing after
        histories will look strange
iron-walking and
        ancient darkness
        drawn-on portraits
drawing your records   on conviction of faces
turning on small
        objections from conscientious
        speaking giants

f   a   u   d   m
  l   y   n   d
i   u   n   y   o
  i   d   n   h

the memory landscape   is ready to explore this
rock   endlessly

18
My crown is in my heart, not on my head; not decked with
diamonds and Indian stones, nor to be seen: my crown
is called content, a crown it is that seldom kings enjoy. [48]

the city linen will work
                    with patchwork-friendly energy
solar light performance in costumes
                    of Shakespeare's Indian republic

17

behind garments
                    to share this regulating critique
and pages to egg
                    talks that people discover accessible
Gaelic sing-songs
                    after spirit-night summer comes to
fourteen transmission routes
up for living work   and neighbour Hinkes

16

brain-write   a story in Mandarin
work individual implications   and
what people look after   in the grass
contemporary traces in   their
source's imaginaries led by   transplantation
post-classic places   as a fresh display
with heritage   at the new

15

exploration is involved in mentalities
and generosity   gathering together outdoors
makes more resources play
                    and dance away full of form
through trauma your comics
                    create hauntings in
                    this physical being outside
non-humans explore landscapes
                    you will walk and work in
Egyptian monuments and other
                    sites of world voice
made pioneering in speakers' contributions to …

14

Dürer's laboratory
meadow woodland campus
        sampling stories
                       back on sound live
followed by deliverances from defence
             begs your responses to this threat
transphobia killings
        from the international abuse
                  in the digital spread
along electronic diagnosis
        surgeons say a robotic trust
               is shaping intelligence
based on tea and bread
           that at the time
               people divided in the city
OK sport   and other focuses

13

suitable chance lantern   before your eyes
a fantastical world of   terrors and winners
and the latest launch of wine   by the comic
will open a river of *being*
               in the poet's eerie home
as a creature found lurking
           on the ludicrously faux-skin
an homage   un-Donne   then

12

improvised piano
a clean fanny beach recovered
               in suitable sea-sailing
inspired by the illustration of
             permanent afternoon
monstrous water-gizmos
        face-up young and fishy
            at new heritage-hub
hand press will sing
       a story cast
           for the local son

11

if you dare enter the copper   propelled by Rose
a sinister land will take form in life
                              as a daydream
what music and fictional events
                       past medicine underpins
refugee performances
          through the personal forces of world
make your language   tell equinox stories

10

enrich how to discover
                 the art villa commonwealth
in which the events of human resilience
                    form magic monsters
and will this water surface surprise
              in pirating an ignoble spirit
imaginative activities of   *being*

9

view the Dude's thoughts
               in the local stops of Rome
at object institutions
        the number will be through the valley
a replica   of the famous bordered place of smell
        to trigger their memories
        to take childhood odours
              into the wild carpet
overpowering an encounter
        with Transylvanian brandy
               of the novel

8

together among silence
         untouched life profits libraries
including inventive   will and home-led host
from others rigour   and engaging debate
from across this   innovative history
in which the
      essential leap-year role will
           highlight the theme

7-6-5

Pat's green river detail
       made foundling surprises Moroccan
that span secrets of snippets   in Cædmon style
and short thoughts
       working throughout industry
a diverse *being*
    in this left out place
       is undertaking
what barriers around us   lead to
a deeper human proposal

4

human form
celebrating curious minds   on secure borders
exploring poetry set across a journey
       and the year we are classical
for its cue and sounds
    as seaside secrets
       turn on location
free exploring for
    being to pick from news
       the showcased

3

the night burns a   patchwork UK in
crimson   sap   ochre   turquoise
    maroon   lime   crimson
violet   orange   blue   and cyan

2

information forum   for body world
the voice of the globe   with a number to spend
but also benefits
    much design and
       a range of philosophies
more first hermit and   wide apart
only special and hosted   in the high-fellow year
for opportunities
    unparalleled in the centre
       of our everyday contribution

for drawing brings bodies together
            to help in guidance across the year
to make the make   with people and the run
in promotion of advanced fun
            to share now in human *being*

1

lfth	I val um	and ia of
and ets we	ose in ome	all out of
me ake ery	ies if me	day

0

| Cut | | around |

1

A tacit ally rules
great softness often comes
                            to cynics trying their lot
exactly a red-headed generation
                    bled like dad had a purpose
kind white people had
                    more arguments for compassion
through that decision
                to credit anti-fascinating things today
together things
        always sense who needs energetic purposes
learning of
            that disadvantageous point
                        at my extreme becoming
I feel more may be asked   of generation change
we hopeful men who   never fought that much
she is reflected   in the granular surprise
in society   and yet in prison
love was   a young
                a young   everything
I doubt
we sacrificed an expensive system
                    when there was a similar crisis
the lower learned the higher case
            that making a letter
                    clearly has sensible profits
puzzled between
        want of perfected techniques
                    and strong nose work
such cynics spot
            the long minority
                        saying of our lifetime
kidnapping words
            make a history   he said
            falling in
            falling in
in which pleasures   admit themselves
            suddenly
as if the enemy of man

can be
            intellectually guilty and
        beautiful
for a long time the loneliness
                to pause when fascinated
said a whopping Atlantic
                might lack the tears of men

2

Guide tankers
imagine there's   the horse of the world
whose introduction
                during the frontline of becoming
translated this love from nature
                distanced by conversations
that sprang from lists
                to artist-drawn kindness

3

Live once
those tough lives   progress to be something
absolutely we've got them opposite
our partners
        the rest have new support to emphasise
inspiration across   more than the capital
years ago we talked normally   training between
domestic abuse   you wouldn't do
the challenge there   to help champions hugely
as need reaches   initiative allows
another drawing of a problem
                the violence is looking for
the partnered parallel it needs   for a solution like
term works from elsewhere
                spanning inspiration cured from
spiralling high across the remarkable letting with
original thinking the real despair
                    is an addiction we need
an essential investment   in poorer people
the idea continues   in someone's biggest panic
those who cut to   mentoring convictions

4

Sabine comic: she ruins passing writer
facing homelessness is
                    that confluence of
                              compassion and hope
would the number of people
                              reframing her idea
truly call that reality into *being*
                    through our experience
their lives transcend the barrier
                    they don't position
to hard people
          resources are bootstraps
                              you can't heck
the results will be inevitable
                              for the judicial system
homelessness insists
          people see a warning
                    and face forward
to choose that context
                    could adjust that spent end
here transformed in
                    earlier landscape scales to
a tight-lipped spin on
                    the shackles of expansion
also the on-looking soar
                without dues
                    to get by in a basic world
where a rough idea played
                    minimum for realists
a universal move forward
                    empowered thought
throughout the same
          inspired handle
                    without maintaining talk
some income is given where
                    enormous influences lift
and transfer the test team
                    of eight years back
often current life
          better prolongs moving
                    in a tirade of dignity

71

believe someone right and whole
                in their move up
                                off the big behind
give no strings to them
                for a people to pocket
                                for that battered room
thanks

5

In the rise wise gods own the freedoms
doomed things and   unjust complacency
                topple scraps of life
                                to pacify the cumulative
repression requires black swathes
                to sow re-orientation
                                                to survive
that is the slave-granting generation
                                to have more members of age
scored on immediate confidence
                                and profound black discourse
whose peers are shallow enough
                in politics to amplify such a world
intensifying years engulfed a rising man
                given life by summer's *ancien régime*
the wreck somehow clearing
                                enough masquerading paradox
a dramatic feeling was stemming
                                the detentions objectively
by means of serious plotting for
                certain long-banned freedoms
but in that decade dictators had
                a momentum particular to the
living fire of a one world narrative
                that hadn't yet come to maintain
the scouring   playing   springs

6

CIVITAS : butch if together mid-lift
to reclaim delicate men's edged words
                                is to make fighting darker
once denial of good reason serves horrors
                                complaining urges others

the movement's great disagreements
        treat secret visions
                as an idyllic infinity
for who refused a night together
           many recovering women
planted awards are also death
           rising to a modern thought
so strong and portcullis white
        that social concerts remain unwritten
        individuals message
        acquaintances lunch
beating campaign fever   across the impossible
segregation
        threatening old actions is
           stressed in personal refuge
however
      convinced without their outrage
          and upsetting my laboratory
memoir against domestic control
          and the awkward book
arson sisters organize
        the non-argued union
           of strange kindness
and defensible reasoning
        remains distinct from
          desirable gentility in methods

7

It is comic in piny houses
gullible old humanity
      is an act that subversive nature
           won't anger tomorrow
but history silences the trust in hierarchy
        when the biggest top goes
then massive trivialities
        equivalent to wartime courage
          switch about
and millions ignite the globe
      in another brutal Floydian prospect
the same terrifying rule is
      far from another weakened justice
now dark easy points are known

                              the great destruction never stills
shaped by more limited evidence
                    we have conservative sentiments
think to eradicate plans and
                    favour the most
                              progressive ever born
almost   progressive enough to
stay the will   of each contribution
                              of supportive parents
realism values   the decades-dropping story
if biology cries
                    each protest is an irony
                              that mankind disciplines
in places that human lies permeate
                    support finds more amazing pundits
the crazy called a major lifetime
                    with this mainstream dismissed
yet almost monthly
                    the notion went higher
                              in the well mind
everything developed
                    through the kick-started platform
becomes the radical world's states
                    that now ignite the justice

8

Adieu hone every mocking army
her airstrike   now hit her eye
bringing   simple conflict   but now
asking
are parties
brutal enough
to pen the peace
the response means
the voices stop calling in   also
thousands brought repairing
from running the everything you   reach
currently rampant supplies   in ruins
of half-backed lives
between long   purge   of peace

9

It hid lugging

heroes know   also belong
bright in life   never sharp
like volatile company
            staying well away from
                        hopeless wounds on masonry
become outdoor orphans
                for dying cattle
                            in dusty peace runs
bloom more frequently
            to make the old country
                                seem southern
at their violence   the group is into

10

No hot pets

you see downhill trouble and
make children run the schools   and humbled
with that deep desire for   solved problems
the places work
and risking a lot   zones protect
standing reasons
to get more from   want
to get better living   abroad with us
now it just founders   on the thinking
energy does in time
everywhere we draw   inspiration
and mark our past less   fortunate

11

Eat hoppy flower

within communities   bravery everywhere
                    this year
focussing prosthetic   fashion assignments

12

Offer goat at start

they deserve   every development together
the key to healthy stress   in each home
is to spend basics   on thousands of books

lives with higher going and less exhaustion result
just one difference
                    made moon furniture
                            for children of the killed
the night consequences of
                        something books provide for
mother income and   old working seizures
boosting an open house   in a single bringing

13

Man below a wage hell
child of my caravans   free the day
bombing off to help sisters   of equal confidence
says the true you   already exists
the struggles they project
                            will be ways to visualize
for everything running in
                        to launch the beautiful from
their emotional
their mental
boys   death-scarred by more
                                old home-years
so proudly raised together in
                            slums of fun tactics
aim for life

14

It's a pure disc, a quaint Shireoaks need
water with nothing over   lost materials
trucked aftermath
where spaces
loved around
the cared-for
help to learn
of operations
process people
witnessed singing
on emotional follow up
the clock could set clean kits   for likes of you
even risk makeshift confusion
from their orphaned many
half a triggered autumn

safe in quake island then
left injured over the province   of measuring

15

Any blither anger
married a million killer
                  and thriving like violence
                                    such a crucial boost
afraid to have   the respected scepticism
also the health
                  to write on equipment
                                    backed by our brothers
decided our learning
joined intervention and   resisted parts of her
with her stricken ideas   ahead but
slums of change   negligible

16

Disk soon bares a … viral direction if born soon
infatuation seems strange
                  thrilling jumpers who think
                                    culture is meeting forward
the point   in the country house
follows the   responding complex   in fortitude
the jokes return there later
                                    over boring air crimes
answers mirror   the encore future
in a remembered cliché   roles agree
disturbance oriented women
suffering loneliness possess depth   awkwardly
trusted in peripheral architecture and   as part-
brand become pheasant invasion specific   to
category
and hardly according to character
emboldened by shock of   drawn-out winter
first sees appeal of meltdown
                  mirrored in our secret career
                                    and polished in rising politics
                                    in dark portraits
placed to fight   such a huge past
to make extraordinary
                  enamoured

day complexes   move on to make good
the doors alongside
              the compelling success
or similarly   in dark months
of found coalitions   just die
we admire the
              festival of current place
                   ending the 1950s   joy tradition
celebrating the world invention
                   of worn media
                   sufficient to   a good moment
in this double-march January   of killing issues

17

He guides creators past rants
prison
prison for false decency
                   ready for the right
                        and unworthy curtain
this remarkable red-leather honour   continues
in ex-academics' exception
in public servants'   responsible listening
but still founded in hope
                        these matters impose little
who will reform thought
who names the conscience   bursting there
insisting that shadow things
                        best distort the word
the tough word
              trying all opted actuals
                        asked to experiment
did the past have obsessions
                   in the scathing   that
together
              have given much to our
                        amazed predecessors
ensuring the short
              director of armed structure
                        escapes accountability
that meddling number of
              higher-scoring professionals
                        constantly work

operational interference   remains the problem
like valid support   masters incompetence
time to buy
     docile military error by
       retired and beloved handshakes
the realm of national projections
       inside the height of organization
useless overall in straight sellers of
     associated balance
and still return to   something broken
       something legend
while imposed
     and as big a fearless has-been
         as says
here in our creaking time
     looks pass through the house
        as once before

18

The pre-forum tests

a)   is the end powerless in prayer who
    seemed laughable of a touting tube
where a socialist exploited hidden wonder
feeling able to imagine lost city frequency
    from fossilized ears listening to
    converted gods of overflowing
empty streets of haunted murmurs awash
with the amulets to a sacred city's love
    to reveal burst nerves on the life
    wanted madness of another where
fabric so utterly new now is born of the
story stirring glows in might and compassion

b)   smart things take to conversation
    tough things to that picked horizon
stay talking brilliant people between slack hope
talk this reasons patience and make eye names
    remember need can introduce the
    same someone thinking within faith
dog ideas might be started but the better result
the real cure a people create looking hardest
    may then benefit surfing such means

of the demonization you count twice
a young suit made lack of disturbing opinion
some life to begin my little fall by something
the young desire found behold green
topping what he went down to question

19

Rage mender
a)   we made this income
serious as our dignity
have many but the shifting
cost might do to freedom
bold in that bank
of the liberated age
would current working
be a genuine subject

b)   imagine the next point
carbon able to move
model thought music away
to become more flexible really
neighbours will be solar
a part-traditional coming
of prospects faster than creating
big bio-role funds playing
early approach beating
more rapidly beating Jim

20

Or at my limit
that future of choice lives
focussed on another jump
backs a much changed god   of scary predictions
what skyrocket conclusions   seem to become
whether what's complete is
simply the painting of time
you get level damage
from this shocking look
and suffered means
call that therapy   but live first   to be saying
bullshit and
ageing infects

                        ageing postpones
exactly the idea   that   it was molecular
an aeroplane
                accumulating processes about
                                        the first forever

21

Hit true office Tues
the separation of futurism
                is polarization to a bubble
                                one housing a zero we feel
and forms of ambition
                are what we holiday from
                                in experimental boom
they might move
                permanent working
                                in legitimate colonies
and engage in talkback
                the auto-face of
                                fashionable structures

22

Putting mental show-round below suave home ambition
run the science first and discover
                                the full glare of the world
they want tough deliberation
                not just nonchalant enthusiasm
they want leaders expressing doubt
                and dedicated outcomes for wimps
zone ambition would be struggling
                                to assume goodwill
under demands   stretched to the
                real centre   of difficulty
a powerful   outside
that takes threatened success of
                important promises in the process
even effective travel   fails the understood
and the concentrated century
                                points to whatever views
that other functioning dichotomy   operates
also   the look really can be hapless
not least in well-fulfilment of   dull opinion

where   only the true is unnecessary
and the hint   is   a perfect think

23
Arms on file
backs dipped
          continually in question
                 unswervingly break
       all special and wrong
wandered off
      to the completely taken fiction
              that isn't liked
to survive a house
      the objectives and interactions
            you imagine well
but for raw stranded structure   to move me
it would be just planning
      on silly position terms and
           propulsion into the real
powerful Hermes principles
      are more advanced
          in our instrumental reality
inventing chunks of commercial effort
          in the real work we do
Mars is something they believe in
that's not about   the reality of organization
how to author a group   based on architecture
one places the importance
          before five years to die
one massive catastrophe right now
      I believe ponders a world played
mark the biggest   again on Earth

24
USA hip to wait
taking the only 'here' in our heads
          construct a start
deal with your own things in bitterness
    even when fully a cheer-point of
         a thoughtful everybody
but our torment is a self-world
      under our attention to a world

you cannot make things
            the philosophy always boils
                fix thinking along other roads to hell
                    however   do they matter
to make an honest aristocracy perfect
                every form shows up
                                all over work
illustration serves as the
                        first guessing imaginary
something written down
                meant more to place
                                the word within
could be an obvious satire
then I thought to write
the wrong information   but why

_____

FINIS

AFTERWORD

Who's been a bad you?
The proposition is a response prompted by Badiou's essay 'Poetry and Communism'.[50]

The political calls for epic poetry. At the same time the 'poem thought' resists a descent into the prosaic, the strictly rational procedure of thinking thought on the page, which is the business of the essay. The point of this resistance is to offer what cannot be said, to offer only what comes into *being* through originary thought. For this, language must be pushed beyond given procedure such as one finds in philosophy, political commentary, literary criticism, etc., at one end of the spectrum, and in instruction, gossip, reportage, etc., at the other. Given procedure—though it is not strict genre adherence in terms of style and form, particularly at the informal end of the spectrum where speech may proceed to flow into and out of events escaping material inscription in the process—is manifest in the play it makes to reconcile the rational and the irrational. To push beyond this play, having no resource but language itself, would seem a paradoxical enterprise. For what does language do but facilitate the (dis)closure of realities made and shared in life? Well, that is indeed the question. To begin to answer one must go back to that notion of the play between the rational and the irrational and note that nothing is said about what falls outside of this play, outside given procedure in general. But one can attach a label to it: what is neither rational nor irrational, what does not fall within the given procedure of language, is the non-rational.

This proposition focuses on the epic not the lyric possibilities of poetry. Arguably the attractions of play remain overwhelming in the lyric, which simplistically one can repeat endlessly as the poetry of love, nature, solitude, meditation, grief, etc., anything but the poetry of war, revolution, slavery, industry ... of worldly endeavour and conflict in general.[51] In my art I have always shied away from the overtly political, that is, from the partisan, the ideological, from explicit positional pronouncement or critique, and I hardly think that is going to change.

I am ill-suited to the activist, socially-engaged, cast of much contemporary artistic practice—I am not a campaigner or a facilitator.[52] The political dimension of activism is usually apparent in its partisan or ideological, and explicit pronouncements. The socially engaged, it seems to me, relies almost entirely on its functional relationship to the state, which is one of sanctioned 'resistance' pressed into supplementary service. Even in its most local form and at its most entrepreneurial, socially-engaged contemporary art practice only gets off the ground under bureaucratic oversight and state-instituted regulation, over which the verdict of the-history-to-come hangs like a spectre. Consequently the institutions are infected with a kind of administrative paranoia and all that matters is pre-validation, legal compliance, and audit trails. I exaggerate a little, but not by much: it is a temperament thing.[53]

Temperamentally I am motivated more as witness, resonator, and scavenger, but in the latter the 'political' is just as much the point. It is just that the political appears there as a prize not a burden, an eye-opening not a brain-binding, a surprise not a given, and the task is to get at it, rather as one gets at the ore of a precious metal hidden deep within the earth, by conducting mining and refining operations. Such operations resist the given procedure of language in which words are present as a legacy that demands judicious exploitation or a heritage that demands reverent recapitulation and irreverent extension. No! Such operations treat words as raw materials to be extracted and worked for their unconstrained possibilities.

I am sure that Aristotle would have understood the principle even though, in his time, there was no reason to attend to its implications. In Greek tragedy the non-rational substance—in Aristotle's terms, the imitation of action[54]—was always delivered via the conventions of narrative play and ritual presentation, i.e. stylized, re-produced speech and behaviour worked on the audience. Too often today convention fails to deliver because its multiplication and contestation in modernism and its subsequent deconstruction and disintegration have largely neutralized this 'viral' potential to work.

Title: the assemblage begins

Badiou references Neruda's epic poem 'Arrival in Madrid of the International Brigade' which is one of 23 poems in his collection *Spain in our Hearts: Hymn to the Glories of the People at War*.[55] Badiou says "This goes to show that the first commitment of the poet is an affective, subjective, immediate solidarity with the Spanish people at war." I like the way that this avoids distinguishing between sympathy—the capacity to resonate with feeling, which requires sensitivity but not understanding—and empathy—the superior capacity for projection of a 'knowing' feeling for the subject—because either can be valid in these terms.

It may come out sounding like propaganda, but that is because (after the fact we can see all too clearly) it is. But then, what 'political' poetry can resist being seen as propaganda eventually? Even Homer's great poems have been offered up by the odd historian "… as evidence for the political forms and structures of late Bronze Age and early Iron Age Greece".[56] Who knows how

86

they were seen at the time? History written by the victors is always going to be t(a)inted; victory must look deserved if not inevitable; we can only fool ourselves it could be otherwise.

Be that as it may, the subtitle of Neurda's poem is my reference point in giving a title to my own for the following reasons, in brief:

Hymn: set aside any Christian connotation and reach back to ancient Greece; to hymn is to sing the praises of. Of what (god) or of whom (which hero) one should sing the praises remains a decision to be made for each occasion and opportunity to open one's mouth. The thought truly is in the singing not the song.

Prisoner: even the astronaut—perhaps the twentieth-century's most mythical hero—is shackled to the earth, because earth is integral to human *being*. Excursion into outer space requires that a minimum of earth goes too: an atmosphere, an embodied materiality, a *being* that continues the sedimentation and erosion of earthly human reality. Gravity rules even in its absence; beyond orbit accelerate close to $9.81 m/s^2$ to feel the uncanny, anything else feels eerily exiling.[57] The star-child is not yet born; that is just a dream, one which only an earth-child can realize from the depths of its cavernous dungeon. Many other 'heroes' are more obviously, and in some cases literally, prisoners; let us sing of them too, if we can find them. True heroes are invested with *Thymos* and have propitious moments in which to act.[58] They strike fear into the souls of the enemy. They affect awe and command respect from all around them. Every true hero is a destroyer-saviour and always operates in the name of a just cause. Modern cynicism claims there are "no more heroes anymore". Perhaps decadence has diminished them because agreement on what is virtuous is no longer possible and their anger therefore cannot be properly directed. Perhaps the wasteland hides its heroes, but they are still there, waiting on a reawakening, on opportunity, and on recognition. Those we dig up may be revealed as no more than shadows of their Greek predecessors, but so what? And what of this wasteland?

Waste Land: maybe the reference here *is* straightforwardly to T S Eliot's long poem. It is a poem that finds its own form through juxtapositions and asymmetries, finds its own sound through plays between assonance, dissonance, and abrupt changes in register, and finds a novel characterization of decadence and despair. It was Eliot's breakthrough 'modernist' poem, but a breakthrough he never really pushed any further. This is not a 'cubist poetry' that deals with simultaneous visual elements such as one finds in William Carlos Williams,[59] but one that orchestrates formally heterogeneous poetic elements to collapse the historical moment. This is Eliot's achievement. *Poiesis* a metaphorical exegesis:

> The Waste Land begins with an ending, *the burial of the dead*, in which one feels surrounded in the company of mourners, each with their own moments of

grief, regret, longing, and private voice, and yet all bearing up (in) the same atmosphere. The historical context suggests that the ending in question was that of the First World War—the poem was written just three years later—but there is also a deeper cultural, wider civilizational, bracket in place for the poem as becomes apparent in its unfolding.

It travels back to the game, *the game of chess*, and a first woman who covers up everything human about her womanhood, and the man who speaks only in the voices of others to avoid speaking at all of pain. Against a second woman that bares it all—flesh, fluids, follies, the body's revenge—is the feeble figurehead of a man with basic needs and objective expectations, and little else except instant recall for the round in the pub and a weight of memory for lost brothers in arms. What do we have? The mundanities. What do we do? We repeat and report and regret, until it is time, time for last orders then time to leave. But escape is not that easy.

It delves into nature's burning heart, *the fire sermon*, desperate by riverside and in boats, fucking, not loving and not repenting, just relieved it is all over when it is done; romance is dead. The land is littered and infested, a degraded scatter of a fragmented heritage swimming in machine-age noise. It seems infertile yet perpetuates a perverse hope of escape, 'perverse' because in the flames of defeat not of purification.

It visits a death, *death by water*, that hope, whatever it was, came to nothing. In water the body bloats, rots, flesh falls from bones; it just diminishes and decays until all that remains are bare bones—metaphor enough for the finesse.

It stops to listen finally and in silence to, *what the thunder said*. Hordes hidden under hoods swarm cities that fall and rise and fall again in a crash, in a flash, history as a blink. No peace for the wicked, and the world prison is just one big wicked problem. It all ends in resignations to be inherited, resignations that will rest tortured souls, free minds to the closures of thought, and keep bodies in the prisons to which they are best suited: school, hospital, field, factory, office, asylum, prison, … capsule(?) in the end there is only the capsule to look forward to; with our cloud memories, server farms, little screens, and tedious gaming in the aether, we are already in training for that foam-form prison.[60]

… and there it grinds to a halt.

The Waste Land is a diminished decaying culture, one which feeds on its past glories in denial of its present enfeebled condition and decimated landscape. The true wasteland of the poem is the modern city, but not just one wasted by war. All that having been said, maybe the 'Waste Land' reference is anything but straightforward; maybe it has little to do with the accident of a centenary and any suggestion of historical, cultural, political, parallels. Yes, all hopes are fossilized in its institutions. All glories are suspended and crimes occulted in its monuments. All atrophying forces are at work. None shall sleep. None shall die. The question is: where is the *Holy Fire* to be found?[61]

On reading

I do not usually read online comments, but I did read one on Wendy Cope's Waste Land Limericks, which suggested that in confronting Eliot's poetry today one person's "arcane pretentiousness" (a damning positive) is another person's "abject failure to communicate" (a considered negative).[62]

I would invert both ideas to support the argument that in confronting Eliot's poetry today, or indeed any other difficult author's poetry, one should embrace promiscuous learning, a shear lust for ideas, and one should immerse oneself in language that operates at the edge of comprehensibility and simply soak it up. There is your cleansing apparatus with which to flush out the dross of the ages and to uncover/recover some primitive connection to the Real and to 'feel' young again, to 'become' young again in one's very *being*.

This quote from Ursula Le Guin:

> Words can be used thus paradoxically because they have, along with a semiotic usage, a symbolic or metaphoric usage. (They also have a sound—a fact the linguistic positivists take no interest in. A sentence or paragraph is like a chord or harmonic sequence in music: its meaning may be more clearly understood by the attentive ear, even though it is read in silence, than by the attentive intellect).[63]

To which I might add that silence is no necessary advantage either: the attentive ear belongs to an entire visceral organism of subtle associated sensitivities any and all of which might be activated by the sound of the words, especially in reading them aloud.

It is important to this poetry—to any poetry as far as I am concerned—to hear it read aloud and to read it aloud yourself. Then you might really experience the physical reverberation and intensification of the poem's five dimensions: graphic, semiotic, symbolic, musical and visceral. In *Hymn to the Prisoners of the Wasteland* a) there is always a stress at or near the beginning of a line, which might be accompanied by touching the air with a clenched fist; b) words that float out to the right, 'sigh' with a falling intonation (although I would not be too bothered by a consistent Aussie or Geordie rising inflection), and the palm of the hand might be lifted with their aspirant sounding; c) the anagrammatic lines/subheads in bold have stresses in each word to sound almost mechanical, which momentary rigidity of head and shoulders might emphasize; and d) the numbers simply mark the division of the poem, so, a slightly longer pause is OK in the reading (they actually number the sections and index the page(s) from which the words are taken in the source publications.) The layout of the text is precise and deliberate—I would love to show it as, and perform it from, a scroll. Its musicality is open to interpretation, of course, but my voicing is consistent throughout. Please do read it (again) aloud.

Epilogue

There is nothing certain in life. The inherited political resignation in the words "but death and taxes" only applies after one has accepted the framework that contains its tautology.[64] Set that aside and one is left with the more primitive, naked, and honest thought[65] that there is an unbridgeable chasm separating the human organism from knowledge of its *predicament*.[66] The beauty of it is that language enables us to have such thoughts as that one and to elaborate them in forms that escape tautology ... in rational discourse, perhaps, and in poetry ... well, it just disappears in poetry of a non-rational flavour.

Reality is not absolute or universal, it is an evolutionary construct based on the technologically enhanced, but still limited, perceptual and cognitive capacities of the organism. As such it shapes behaviour in ways that keep the species surviving and in many respects thriving. There is nothing certain, no one and only 'Truth', to underpin a functional reality: think about it, there can't be. Truth would entail final information, all of it, all at once, and the overload would be lethal to the organism, an evolutionary terminus.[67]

No, the functional reality is a web of necessary illusions, which inherited resignations enable us to take for granted. Art—the real thing that is—is the process that renders illusion absolutely present as such. If you are open to art you allow yourself to be sensitized to reality's fragile contingencies. This may not make us "better, nicer, happier" or fitter, but maybe it makes us more alive.[68]

14 February 2021

ENDNOTES

1   Gilbert Adair and I reacquainted ourselves with Burroughs' Word-virus routine during our discussion of 'Language in the reality making operation', see: following note.

2   'Language in the reality making operation' parts 1, 2, 3 and 4 on the blog pages of The Centre for Experimental Ontology: <https://centreforexperimentalontology.com>

3   Source: *RSA Journal*, issue 3, 2020. Pages for each section as follows: 1, p. 50; 2, pp. 48-9; 3, pp. 44-7; 4, pp. 42-3; 5, pp. 40-1; 6, pp. 36-9; 7, p. 35; 8, pp. 32-3; 9, pp. 28-31; 10, pp. 22-7; 11, pp. 20-1; 12, pp. 16-19; 13, pp. 10-15; 14, p. 9; 15, p. 8; 16, p.7; 17, p.6; 18, pp. 4-5; and 19, p. 3.

4   T S Eliot. The Waste Land, V, lines 7-9.

5   Florence Nightingale, letter to Mary Clark, 1844 quoted in: Edward Tyas Cook *The Life of Florence Nightingale*, Vol. 1, (1914, London: Macmillan).

6   George Orwell. *1984*.

7   Sophocles. *Oedipus Rex*, trans. F. Storr.

8   Dennis M. Mares. Civilization, economic change, and trends in interpersonal violence in western societies, *Theoretical Criminology*, Vol. 13, No. 4, p. 442.

9   Quoted in: Jennifer P. Wisdom, et al. 'Stealing Me from Myself': Identity and Recovery in Personal Accounts of Mental Illness, *Australian & New Zealand Journal of Psychiatry*, 1 January 2008.

10 Colossians 3:5, King James Bible.

11 In the book of Daniel (King James Bible) the 35th word is "saying" and then he recounts the dream in which four great beasts emerge from the sea.

12 Michael Drayton. *Poly-Olbion*, 18:735-6. <http://poly-olbion.exeter.ac.uk/the-text/full-text/song-18> accessed 6 January 2021.

13 John Hawks quoted in: Maya Wei-Haas. Controversial new study pinpoints where all modern humans arose, *National Geographic*, updated 5 November 2020 <https://www.nationalgeographic.co.uk/history-and-civilisation/2019/10/controversial-new-study-pinpoints-where-all-modern-humans-arose> accessed 6 January 2021.

14 From letter no. 23, in Ortelius, A. (geographer Sanensis) letters and discussions compiled and edited by J. H. Hessels (1887, Cambridge). Quoted in English from: Grossmann. 'Bruegel's "Woman Taken in Adultery" and other grisailles', *The Burlington Magazine*, XCIV (Aug., 1952), p. 226.

15 Jeremy Deller interviewed by Hettie Judah <https://inews.co.uk/culture/jeremy-deller-i-dont-make-art-to-relax-grayson-perry-art-club-thank-god-for-immigrants-poster-428422> accessed 6 January 2021

16 William Shakespeare. *A Midsummer Night's Dream*, Act 2, Scene 1.

17 Gilbert Adair, hh Parlement of Foules, from **h c e,** manuscript dated 3 January 2021. In the greater Eleusinian Mysteries the initiate walks to the sea to be cleansed.

18 C L R James. *My friends: a fireside chat on the war* (1940, New York: Workers Party).

19 Allen Fisher. Confidence in Lack, 2007, <https://allenfisher1.files.wordpress.com/2010/08/allen-fisher-confidence-in-lack.pdf> accessed 7 January 2021.

20 Ursula Le Guin. A Palindrome I Do Not Want To Write (2009), <https://www.ursulakleguin.com/the-palendromedary> accessed 6 January 2021

21 Quoted in: Germano Celant. *Beuys, tracce in Italia* (1978, Napoli: Amelio).

22 Peter Sloterdijk. *Critique of Cynical Reason*, trans. Michael Eldred (1987, Minneapolis: University of Minnesota Press), p. 49.

23 John Cage. Composition as Process, in: *Silence: Lectures and Writings* (1973, Hanover, NH: University Press of New England), p. 47.

24 Paul Celan. 'The Meridian' speech, 1960.

25   *Greenpeace Connect*, summer 2019, pp. 30-1.

26   There are always Biblical echoes, see: 1 Corinthians 10:12, but I was reading: Thomas Moynihan. *Spinal Catastrophism* (2019, Falmouth: Urbanomics), p. 111 ff.

27   See my poem: Sônia, dated 17 Nov 2020. Sources: *Greenpeace Connect*, Winter 2020, p. 14, and Peter S. Wells, *How Ancient Europeans Saw the World* (2012, Prineton NJ/Oxford: Princeton University Press), pp. 222-9.

28   Source: Markus Mauthe. 'Rescuing the Amazon,' in *Greenpeace Connect*, Summer 2020, pp. 20-3.

29   William Shakespeare. *Macbeth*, Act V, scene VIII.

30   "… in the forests of the night" William Blake. The Tyger.

31   Dragon Endeavour release mechanism from the International Space Station; the Demo-2 mission returned on 2 August 2020.

32   Lucius Livius Andronicus (c. 284 – c. 205 BC) first translator of Homer's *Odyssey* into Latin.

33   In Welsh, Wthyr Bendragon, legendary king of sub-Roman Britain and the father of King Arthur.

34   Sources: J. Sauven. 'Vision', *Greenpeace Connect*, Summer 2020, p. 2, and R. Snailham. 'Appendix D: Nick Cooke's Citation' in *Sangay Survived: The Story of the Ecuador Volcano Disaster* (1978, London: Hutchinson & Co.) pp. 187-8.

35   T S Elliot was 22 when he wrote '… Prufrock' and in 1976 I was 22 and being a bit of a Prufrock.

36   Sources: *Greenpeace Connect*, Spring 2020; János Manga. *Herdsmen's art in Hungary* (1972, Budapest: Corvina Press); and Fred Hoyle. *The Black Cloud* (1957, London: Heinemann). Note on process: a) reverse decimations interleaved 1,2,3: 1,2,3: etc., b) 1,2,3 intrications, c) elaborations and cuts, and d) format.

37   William Burroughs. *The Ticket That Exploded* (2010, London: Fourth Estate) p. 40.

38   Source: *Greenpeace Connect*, Autumn 2018.

39   Source: *Greenpeace Connect*, Spring 2020.

40   Source: *Museums Journal*, November/December 2020. Pages for each section as follows: 1, p. 60; 2, p. 63; 3, p. 62; 4, p. 61; 5, pp. 59-61; 6, pp. 58-9; 7, p. 54; 8, pp. 50-3; 9, pp. 46-9; 10, pp. 42-4; 11, pp. 36-7; 12, pp. 32-5; 13, pp. 29-31; 14, pp. 24-6; 15, p. 21; 16, pp. 18-20; 17, pp. 8-9; 18, p. 6; 19, pp. 4-5; and 20, p. 3.

41   See: 'Catalyse', a poem I drafted on 9 November 2020.

42   Source: Being Human: A Festival of the Humanities, brochure, 14-23 November 2019.

43   Barbara Kingsolver. *Animal, Vegetable, Miracle: A Year of Food Life* (2007, London: Faber & Faber), p. 26.

44   Charles Dickens. *A Tale of Two Cities*, No Fear: Bk. 3, Ch. 13. "In the black prison of the Conciergerie, the doomed of the day awaited their fate. They were [etc.]"

45   "How would Lucia's last words do? 'Just wait till we come back.'" E. F. Benson. *Mapp and Lucia*, ch.10. There is a real Riseholme, of course, 3km due north of Lincoln Cathedral.

46   We need heroes not saints, then the sentiment is reversed and reversed again; it never resolves.

47   Roy Flechner (ed.) Concerning dissolving an oath and, on the contrary, not dissolving it, *The Hibernensis*, vol. 2. (2019: Washington DC: Catholic University of America), 66:7, p. 831.

48   William Shakespeare. *King Henry VI*, Act III, Scene I.

49   Sources: Rutger Bregman (ed.) Cynicism is out, hope is in, *The Big Issue*, No. 1426, 7 September 2020, pp. 16-29: pages for each section: 1, pp. 26-9; 2, p. 24; 3, p. 23; 4, pp. 20-1; 5, p. 19; 6, p. 18; and 7, pp. 16-7. *Children Now: Special Centenary Issue*, 2019, Save the Children UK: pages for each section: 8, p. 20; 9, p. 19; 10, p. 18; 11, p. 17; 12, p. 15; 13, pp. 12-14; 14, pp. 10-11; and 15, pp. 8-9. *The Big Issue*, No. 1156, 1 June 2015: pages for each

section: 16, pp. 25-7; and 17, pp. 20-3. Utopia Special, *The Big Issue*, No. 1191, 8 February 2016: pages for each section: 18, pp. 26-7; 19, pp. 24-5; 20, p. 23; 21, p. 21; 22, pp. 20-21; 23, pp. 18-9; and 24, p. 17.

50   Badiou, *The Age of the Poets*, p. 93-108.

51   I use 'epic' and 'lyric' in artificially distinct ways here. This reflects my fringe relationships to the Classics, to English literature, and to any idea of an American or (in translation) a European canon. I came to literature later in life and I am no scholar. I don't apologise for this, merely stress that the emphasis I put on certain general qualities of the epic and the lyric—i.e. long v short, sentiment v story, intensive v extensive, circularity v linearity, etc.,— provide a suitably solid, if naïve, schema to (under)mine in what I produce. As an artist with primarily material and procedural motivations, and a healthy disinterest in allegiances, I feel completely at liberty to operate in this way. Call me a despicable opportunist if you wish … it's a point of view.

52   I taught the theory and practice of exhibition design for nearly thirty years (1986-2015) but resolutely within museological and brand communications arenas that remained largely unaffected by the innovations of contemporary artistic practice until very late in the day. The activism and social engagement of many artists made cross-disciplinary practice in exhibition 'making' inevitable, of course, but I am glad that as an academic I did not have to deal with the new problematics that have arisen as a consequence.

53   From the beginning of my academic career this 'temperament' was apparent. As a lecturer I was motivated to undertake a PhD because I needed to make sense of my preceding six-year experience of working in a national museum—almost an exemplar of the kind of institution that all too easily becomes infected with administrative paranoia: "Mature organizations, institutions like the museum, tend to become primarily concerned with self-perpetuation and only secondarily concerned with their supposedly principal purposes, even if these are evolving." Add that on to my prior experience of obtaining funding for an art project from a Regional Arts Association: "By 1979 … I had had my first encounter with the bureaucracy and, as far as I could see, the blindness and corruption of regional arts administration, and I needed to get out." And you can see why my 'kynical' attitude may have been fostered in the research [quotes from my PhD thesis: *Museum·Design·Organization* (1996, University of Hull) p. 5, & p. 2.]

54   In comparing poets Aristotle observes that: πράττοντας γὰρ μιμοῦνται καὶ δρῶντας ἄμφω. "… they both represent *men in action* and *doing things*." (emphasis added: the latter can be mimicked and reproduced, the former however requires transmission of an affection, the viral effect of poetry). [Aristotle, *Poetics*, 1448a: 4]

55   Pablo Neruda. *Spain in Our Hearts: Espana En El Corazon*, trans. Donald D. Walsh (2005, New York: New Directions Bibelot.)

56   David F. Elmer. Poetry's politics in archaic Greek epic and lyric, *Oral Tradition*, vol. 28 no. 1, pp. 143-66, (p. 144.)

57   On the experience of microgravity in orbit Sergey Ryazansky. "During the first two weeks we have bruises." Another effect: "the tops of your feet grow calluses, and the calluses that were once on the bottom disappear." Getting taller, puffy face, skinny legs, loss of coordination, muscle atrophy, crumbling bones, restlessness; in no particular order these are just the beginning of an absolute alienation. <https://www.washingtonpost.com/graphics/2019/national/50-astronauts-life-in-space> accessed 20 February 2021.

58   *Thymos*: virtuous anger. For Homer the word had broad psychological meanings. In Plato's *Republic* and *Phaedrus* it is associated with "a pared-down model of human agency". But it is Aristotle who generally uses the word "as a synonym for *orgē* (anger) [with] … traces of older associations between *thymos* and qualities such as assertiveness and goodwill towards

others." (*Oxford Classical Dictionary* <https://oxfordre.com/classics/view/10.1093/acrefore/9780199381135.001.0001/acrefore-9780199381135-e-8180 >) Peter Sloterdijk discusses the concept at length in: *Rage and Time: A Psychopolitical Investigation*, trans. Mario Wenning (2010, New York: Columbia University Press).

59   See: Jan-Louis Kruger. William Carlos Williams' cubism: The sensory dimension, *Literator* vol. 16, no. 2, August 1995, pp. 195-213.

60   "The closest discipline to this heterodox theory of culture and civilization is presently that of manned space travel: nowhere else is there such radical enquiry into the technical conditions of possibility of human existence in life-sustaining capsules." Peter Sloterdijk. *Foams: Spheres,* volume 3, trans. Wieland Hoban (2016, South Pasadena CA: Semiotext(e)), p. 37.

61   This refers to a radical rejuvenation therapy, which preserves memory and peak cognitive functions while turning back the biological clock in every cell of the body to extend life indefinitely. Bruce Sterling. *Holy Fire* (1996, London: Orion).

62   The source may as well remain anonymous as it is littered with anachronistic errors.

63   Ursula Le Guin. Introduction, in *The Left Hand of Darkness* (1976, New York: Ace Books).

64   "'Tis impossible to be sure of any thing but Death and Taxes" (1716) Christopher Bullock. *The Cobler of Preston, a farce. As it is acted at the Theatre-Royal in Lincoln's-Inn-Field*, 5th edn. (1767, London: Bladon), p. 21. Although the later quotation taken from Benjamin Franklin's letter to Jean-Baptiste Le Roy (1789) is the more famous: "Our new Constitution is now established, and has an appearance that promises permanency; but in this world nothing can be said to be certain, except death and taxes." Farce as politics, politics as farce; take your pick.

65   The echo of W S Burroughs there is from the screenplay of *Naked Lunch* (David Cronenberg (dir.) film, 1991). In the second scene, set in a café, two young writers, Hank and Martin, argue about whether or not to edit and rewrite; the key line is spoken by Hank. "Well, how about guilt re: censoring your best thoughts? Your most honest, primitive, real thoughts …"

66   I mean this in the modern sense, but with the thickness of Aristotle's Κατηγορίαι.

67   See: Fitness-Beats-Truth Theorem in: Donald D Hoffman, *The Case Against Reality* (2019, London: Allen Lane), p. 61ff.

68   I am responding to Michael Blackburn here; in our video piece *Art Land* (2005) he asks "What would you do … [if you] experienced art that didn't make you a better, nicer, happier person, but did the opposite …?"
     <https://www.youtube.com/watch?v=whDf1y1h9e8> accessed 27 January 2021.

www.ingramcontent.com/pod-product-compliance
Lightning Source LLC
Chambersburg PA
CBHW021936040426
42448CB00008B/1099